W9-BCI-319

Sanctifying Truth

Romanus Cessario, O.P.

Sanctifying Truth

Thomas Aquinas on Christian Holiness

MAGNIFICAT

Paris • New York • Oxford • Madrid

Publisher: Romain Lizé
Copyeditor: Susan Needham
Iconography: Isabelle Mascaras
Layout: Julia Pateu
Cover: Gauthier Delauné
Production: Pierre Macqueron
Proofreading: Samuel Wigutow
Front cover: *Saint Thomas Aquinas*, Antonio Rodriguez (1636-1691), National
            Museum of Art, Mexico City, Mexico. © Bridgeman Images.

Copyright © 2021 by MAGNIFICAT Inc. All rights reserved.

Printed in 2021 by Imprimerie Marquis, Canada
First edition: May 2021
Edition number: INT2101
ISBN: 978-1-949239-82-9

No part of this book may be used or reproduced in any manner whatsoever without
written permission, except in the case of brief quotations embodied in critical
articles or reviews. For information, address MAGNIFICAT, PO Box 834, Yonkers,
NY 10702. www.magnificat.com

For
Ryan Wilson Connors
Priest & Friend

Sed nec benevolentia sufficit
ad rationem amicitiae,
sed requiritur quaedam mutua amatio,
quia amicus est amico amicus.

Summa theologiae II-II q. 23, art. 1

Contents

PREFACE

⊰∘⊱⊰∘⊱⊰∘⊱

Many saints, even those who have been canonized by the Church, remain hidden in the yellowing pages of sacred books. Thomas Aquinas, however, ranks among those saints who enjoy worldwide name recognition. In the course of their lives, most Catholics and many others have heard about this thirteenth-century scholar, theologian, and mystic. Students in many disciplines also come across the adjectival form of his name and the name of his school. This happens when they encounter something or someone described as Thomist. Even the substantive, Thomism, has become familiar to scholars, not only of philosophy and theology, but also of law, art, and literature.

Saint Thomas Aquinas's reputation as a medieval scholar unfortunately persuades many Christians that only theologically educated people will find anything of spiritual worth in his life and work. This small book proposes to show that

Thomas Aquinas appears as a saint for all Christians, whatever the interests or abilities each believer may possess. The Church indeed recognizes in Thomas Aquinas a man of extraordinary intellectual accomplishments. At the same time, because his searching for and pondering of divine truth sanctified him, the Church proclaimed Thomas Aquinas a saint. Many study theology, but only holy scholars illumine the Church with their teachings.

It is not easy to write about the saints, especially about one of such spiritual density as Thomas Aquinas. The ensuing pages aim to illustrate the principal lessons from his life and writings that will prove helpful to all Christians. In particular, Thomas's teaching leads us through the following line of argumentation: Since God is the supreme and first truth ("*summa et prima veritas*," *ST* I q. 16, art. 5), divine truth sanctifies those who embrace it. Study affords the best approach to this embrace; the person who loves the truth he studies and who ponders it in his heart, that one becomes a contemplative. Then, the highest qualities that adorn human life animated by divine grace appear as charity and wisdom. Though not first among the moral virtues, chastity (sexual passion that has been well-tempered) supports the other virtues; the unchaste person finds it difficult to develop prudence, justice, and fortitude, as well as the other virtues associated with temperance. Certainly, moral virtue in general remains necessary for the Christian who wishes to observe a contemplative pace throughout life. Indeed, humility occupies a foundational role in the development of the Christian virtues, even though this virtue falls among the least of the cardinal moral virtues. Contemplation brings both an ardent devotion toward and a deepened understanding of the mysteries of the Christian religion. The more one grows in simplicity of spirit, the better he or she is disposed to receive this grace of sanctifying truth.

This book appears in the fiftieth year of my priestly ordination, which occurred on 27 May 1971. From the day on which, a few years before my ordination, I received the same black and white habit that Thomas Aquinas wore, this saintly older brother in the Order of Saint Dominic has been for me a source of both intellectual and spiritual nourishment. I therefore gratefully acknowledge those Dominicans as well as many good lay people who have fostered my love for and understanding of Saint Thomas Aquinas.

Friendship, as Aquinas himself teaches, arises from a mutual sharing of something. Father Ryan Connors, a priest of the Diocese of Providence, Rhode Island, has shared his love for Saint Thomas's teachings with me, his students, and his parishioners. This good and courageous priest also demonstrates the truthfulness of what Aquinas says about friendship, "it is only with a friend that a friend is friendly" (*Summa theologiae* II-II, q. 23, art. 1). So at the completion of the fifth decade of my priesthood, I gladly dedicate this book to Father Connors in the first of his.

WISDOM
AND WISDOM'S FRUITS

> For never has anyone studied,
> in the right spirit, the writings of Thomas
> without receiving abundance of knowledge
> and wisdom and wisdom's fruits.
> The spiritual flood of his teachings
> has both increased the wisdom of the wise
> and nourished the minds of little ones.
>
> Bernard Gui, "Life of St. Thomas Aquinas," 12*

On 28 January each year, Catholics throughout the world honor Thomas Aquinas. It happens that this date, 28 January, marks the day in 1367 when the relics of Saint Thomas arrived in solemn procession at the outskirts of Toulouse. The Avignon pope, Urban V, had been a student of the Dominicans in this French city situated on the banks of the Garonne. It was Pope Urban who had made the decision to house the relics of the recently canonized Friar Thomas d'Aquino in the French Midi instead of in Paris, where Thomas had made his name as a theologian, or at Naples, where he had attained his maturity and had entered the then

* The epigraphs that immediately follow each chapter heading come from Bernard Gui, "The Life of St. Thomas Aquinas," contained in *The Life of Saint Thomas Aquinas: Biographical Documents*, trans. & ed. K. Foster (London: Longmans, Green & Co., 1959). The numbers refer to the enumeration in Gui's medieval work.

newly founded Friars Preachers or Dominicans. Since Thomas's death almost a century before, on 7 March 1274, his body had been in the possession of the Cistercian monks of Fossanova, the Italian abbey where Thomas died while journeying north from Naples toward Lyons to serve as a *peritus* at the fourteenth ecumenical council, known as Second Lyons.

Liturgical feasts of course celebrate more than past events. We venerate the saints because they are alive today in Christ. In the case of Thomas Aquinas, the Church venerates him as her Common Doctor. Many official texts confirm this title, but the *Code of Canon Law*, paragraph 252, suffices to establish Aquinas's preeminent place among the Doctors of the Christian Church. The *Code* invokes his name in the ablative absolute, *sancto Thoma praesertim magistro*, when it ordains that students learn about the mysteries of salvation—Saint Thomas, especially, being the *magister*, the master.[1] In other words, Saint Thomas enjoys primacy of place as a guide to the study of theology.

Oftentimes we find the image of Saint Thomas placed among those of the ancient Fathers of the Church, those Doctors of the Church from both East and West whom the Church recognizes as the carriers of the apostolic tradition: Saints Ambrose,

Augustine, Gregory the Great, and Jerome from the West; Saints Athanasius, Basil the Great, Gregory Nazianzen, and John Chrysostom from the East.[2] During the period that followed the Catholic Reform of the sixteenth century, images of the Doctors of the Church became a standard decoration in Catholic churches. Local artists copied what they found in Saint Peter's Basilica in Rome. Today one may still see the images of the four Fathers who hold up the gilt bronze casing designed by Gian Lorenzo Bernini to encase the Chair of Peter. It was executed during the years between 1647 and 1653. The pope at that time, Alexander VII, surely wanted to make his theological message clear. All that the popes teach enjoys continuity with the doctrine of the eight great teachers of Catholic antiquity who themselves enjoy continuity with the apostles and so are revered as the original "Doctors of the Church."

The Protestant Reform contested this tradition. Martin Luther and his followers held a different view of the history of the Catholic Church. They opined that from the time that the last drop of ink had dried on the pages of the New Testament, the Roman Church and the pope of Rome managed to get everything wrong. Nothing was right. Everything required fixing. The Protestant Reform enacts then the first large-scale doctrinal rupture with the past, the first modern example of applying the hermeneutics of discontinuity to Catholic thought and practice. The divines of the sixteenth-century Reform further detested Aquinas and what they derisively called scholastic theology.

Why does Saint Thomas find an iconographic place among the Doctors of the Church? The answer is easy. He is the first teacher of Catholic doctrine after the patristic period to receive officially, in 1567, the title "Doctor of the Church." Pope Saint Pius V, another Dominican, declared him so four years after the close of the reforming Council of Trent, at which Thomas Aquinas clearly served as the Church's *Doctor Communis*. This pope himself had studied closely the works of Aquinas, so he knew that Aquinas was a carrier of the Tradition, and he knew that the Protestant Reformers were wrong to reject him. More recently, in his 1879 landmark encyclical *Aeterni Patris*, Pope Leo XIII set forth Aquinas as a sure guide for Catholic theology and philosophy. To interpret these developments within the Church, we need only to recall the principle of continuity that Pope Benedict XVI once urged the Church to observe.[3] The Fathers and Aquinas exhibit continuity with the divine revelation that the evangelists and apostles bequeathed to their successors who are the bishops.

In his 1995 Encyclical Letter, *Fides et ratio*, Pope Saint John Paul II observed that Thomas Aquinas welcomed truth on its own terms and from whatever source it came, and the pope encouraged others to follow that example.[4] Aquinas's deployment of Aristotelian philosophy provides a good example of his inclusiveness. Why does the Church hold Aquinas in such high esteem? There are many reasons. Let me single out one that reveals his importance for both Christian theology and Christian living. I refer to Aquinas's genius for taking the world seriously. The late German philosopher Josef Pieper once remarked that, just as the Little Flower, known as Thérèse of the Child Jesus, received the title "of the Child Jesus," so Aquinas should have been called Brother Thomas of the Creator—*Thomas a Creatore*.[5] Why? Aquinas's profound respect for the created order distinguishes his work from much of the symbolic theology that preceded him. It also sets him apart from those who today refuse to recognize that created natures of various kinds fall under the purview of the theologian, who must treat the God who is the Creator of all things visible and invisible.

Respecting as he does the truth of things, *veritas rerum*, Aquinas is able to distinguish without separating the orders of nature and of grace, and this allows him to illuminate the specific ways in which God acts in each order. In the first, God is the creating and sustaining cause of all that exists, such that without his immediate, sustaining presence no creature remains in being, whereas in the second order, that of divine grace, God transforms intelligent yet dependent creatures into his good friends. The Church esteems Aquinas's proper respect for created natures within the larger outpouring of divine grace. She recognizes that people are drawn to a gospel message that transforms them from within the human natures that they possess. Christ of course commits the Church to the work of evangelization: "Go into the whole world and proclaim the gospel to every creature" (Mk 16:15). That promise given to every human creature who accepts the gospel appears as a divinization of their human natures.

It may come as a surprise to some readers that between 1654 and 1678, the *Summa theologiae* was published twice in Peking (Beijing), having been translated into Chinese by two Jesuit missionaries. More recently, a Salesian missionary preparing to serve in China asked permission to publish in

Chinese more than a few pages of a book that outlines the history of Thomism.[6] One may interpret this somewhat remarkable request as an indication of just how much Aquinas fulfills still the role of Common Doctor. The seventeenth-century missionaries undoubtedly concluded that Aquinas's openness to the world of creation made his writings of potential interest to the men and women of all cultures. They were not the first to draw this conclusion. Shortly after the death of Aquinas, the Dominican authorities in 1274 received a letter from the Faculty of Arts (which was a faculty of Philosophy) at the University of Paris. The authors first lamented the loss of a brilliant teacher: "Truly it is as though the sun had withdrawn its splendor or suffered the overshadowing of an untimely eclipse, now that this light of the Church is put out."[7] However, these Parisian masters had a more practical objective at hand. They wanted copies of Aquinas's philosophical writings about which they had heard. So they reminded the Dominicans about Aquinas's interest in nature. "It was," they went on to say, "by a special privilege that the Creator of Nature willed to concede this light for a time to the world." Then they made an even bolder assertion in order to persuade the Dominicans of the rightness of their requests. "It seemed," they further wrote, "that Nature herself had placed this man here amongst us to shed light on her own mysteries." About 750 years later, there are many Thomist achievements that support this view of the Parisian masters in Arts, among which the seventeenth-century Chinese editions of the *Summa* especially stand out.

Aquinas encourages all Catholics to take study seriously. The Thomist approach to contemplation and study dominates the Catholic reform movement of the sixteenth century—the same period that witnesses Aquinas's being named a Doctor of the Church. The Catholic Reform was instigated at the Council of Trent, which, as the Dominican historian Guy Bedouelle observes, "agreed to conjoin doctrine and discipline, theology and practice, contemplation and action, and perhaps (even if this seems paradoxical to some) the temporal and the spiritual."[8] In short, a reform that took up the deeply Catholic intuitions that Aquinas enshrined in his large *corpus* of writing.[9] No either-or approach for Catholics. Faith or works? Scripture or Tradition? Grace or freedom? Instead, the Catholic outlook on Christian life is always "both-and." The history of Catholic theology since the sixteenth century confirms that "both-and" theology poses a difficult subject to master. Still, master it the intelligent

Catholic must. To cite some particulars: Christ, God *and* man. The Church, human *and* divine. Sacraments, signs *and* causes. The priest, Father X *and* another Christ. Forgiveness *and* Confession. The list goes on.

Study for the Catholic remains a contemplative act. We do not pursue studies only to discover the knack of doing this or that. We do not undertake study only to develop the high-end skills of management or technology, even when these may be put at the service of worthwhile endeavors. We do not ponder divine truth so that we can acquit ourselves of professional responsibilities as Catholic believers. In the final analysis, Catholics study so they can pray. To be sure, it is certain that the study of the divine sciences and the practice of contemplative prayer flow from that single act of divine faith whereby we accept the truth about God. As for the philosophical sciences and all that derives from them, including the natural sciences, the same contemplative approach applies. For the educated Catholic, contemplative study provides the inexhaustible and irreplaceable source of everything that he or she does. No short cuts are available. No one is exempt. One may construe study broadly. Study does not require necessarily engagement in formal education. Spiritual books, the lives of the saints, the liturgical texts for the daily Mass all supply rich sources of divine truth that everyone may ponder studiously. Whatever form study may take, the applying of oneself to the study of divine truth affords the only way for the Catholic believer to discover and to remember that God remains the Lord of all learning and that all learning leads back to him, *Deus Scientiarum Dominus*—God, the Master of all sciences.[10]

The Council of Trent stressed the unity of theology and practice, contemplation and action, but other ecclesial forces within the modern period have found it convenient to separate them. Practice of the Christian life is one thing, they have argued, whereas study is another—a pragmatic option taken up in order that its proponents might achieve certain goals. History, though, demonstrates that the separation of contemplation from study leaves both weakened. Uninstructed piety can produce purported visionaries, misled mystics, or religious enthusiasts. On the other hand, savants who do not pray fall victim to academic fads and may even succumb to secular ideologies. Saint Thomas would not have recognized this pragmatic approach to study. For educated Catholics especially, the separation of study and prayer oftentimes brings catastrophic results inasmuch as their minds lead them away from the truth instead of toward its embrace.

Thomas Aquinas knew that contemplative study does not come easily. Like every good action, study requires a virtuous formation to ensure that our study achieves the desired effect. In a letter traditionally attributed to Aquinas, he explained to one of his contemporary Dominican friars how to begin the adventure of the intellectual life: "Because you have asked me, John, my dearest friend in Christ, how you should study to amass the treasure of knowledge, such is the advice I give to you. You should choose to enter not immediately into the ocean depths, but rather through small streams, for one should reach more difficult matters by going through the easier ones first."[11] This counsel should not alarm the Christian who wants to make study of spiritual things a daily practice. The Christian tradition offers up an enormous body of spiritual literature—much of it from the pens of saints—that provides material for contemplative study. What matters most to the beginner comes in the form of a promise that the witness of Saint Thomas Aquinas makes plainly evident. Divine truth not only informs, it also sanctifies. The more we ponder saving truth, the more we grow in the holiness of life that Aquinas himself exhibits in a remarkable way. Still, Aquinas's advice to Brother John holds true: take one step at a time.

The following chapters should inform about the life of Aquinas and at the same time, in God's Providence, also edify the benevolent reader, who will discover therein the riches of Aquinas's holiness. The lesson that applies to both beginners and the advanced remains the same: the embrace of divine truth possesses the capacity to sanctify. To put it differently, only the truth has grace.

A LOVE OF THE DOCTRINE
OF SALVATION

And surely it was appropriate,
that in this way Providence
should indicate in the boy what was to be
so conspicuous in the man,
a love of the doctrine of salvation
which it would be his vocation to teach.
It was the divine Spirit that led him to that paper.

Gui, "Life," 2.

Who would begin a life of Francis of Assisi without describing the Umbrian hilltown that *il Poverello* has made famous? Likewise no one should commence a biographical sketch of Thomas Aquinas without mentioning the town located on a sunny plain in the Lazio region of Italy from which he receives his surname. Aquino on the Via Latina stands halfway between Rome and Naples. The town's origin reaches back to the peninsula's pre-Christian history, and at least by the end of the sixth century the municipality had become the seat of a Catholic bishopric. The fortitude required to endure repeatedly invading barbarians and bloody conflicts waged in and around Aquino, including a significant Allied victory on 23 March 1944, long ago developed a resiliency in the Aquinati, who today number more than 5,000 souls. If there is one common feature of Thomas's life and work, it is resilience. That quality distinguishes not only the person of Thomas Aquinas but also his vast literary output, especially the *Summa theologiae*. Further, the commentatorial tradition that authentically interprets Aquinas's teachings manifests the resiliency noted in the master himself.

Although some claim that Thomas Aquinas was born within the confines of medieval Aquino, both a long tradition and reliable scientific research favor another location close by.[12] Since it reveals the pride (and perhaps envy) that Thomas begets in his neighbors and family, the dispute merits a brief recall. In 1961, the Thomist historian Angelo Walz, O.P., reported that no fewer than four Italian cities have laid claim to the honor of being the birthplace of Saint Thomas Aquinas: Belcastro in Calabria (whose assertion rests on fraudulent documents), Naples (because of a sixteenth-century commemorative epigraph that speaks of "Thomas de Aquino Neapolitanus"), the above-mentioned Aquino, and a place called Roccasecca.[13] The earliest documentation clearly indicates the latter site as Thomas's birthplace. There a fortress-castle still sits (in ruins) on a craggy mountainous elevation (thus, "dry rock") below Monte Asprano.

This medieval stronghold belonged to the noble family of Thomas d'Aquino. His earliest biographer, William di Tocco (d. c. 1322), reports that a hermit named Bonus, who dwelt within the rough terrain of the region, visited this residence of the Aquino nobles to inform Thomas's mother, Theodora, that the child in her womb would accomplish great deeds for the Church.[14] This Tocco, who interviewed members of Saint Thomas's family in order to acquire information about the saint's early life, goes on to relate that the toddler Thomas exhibited the qualities of any young boy. For example, once during the course of his receiving a bath, the family nanny found Thomas clenched-fisted, tenaciously holding onto a piece of paper—as children of a certain age are wont to do. To the surprise of all, however, baby Thomas's scrap of paper that he had picked up from the floor contained the words "Hail Mary!"[15] As the epigraph above shows, a fourteenth-century hagiographer like Bernard Gui would demur from the thought that this charming story lacked significance for the saint's future calling in life.

During the Middle Ages, schooling by and large remained under the auspices of clerics, especially of monks in monasteries. It is difficult to underestimate, as scholars like Christopher Dawson have pointed out, the importance that Benedictine monasteries played in the rise of Western culture. When Thomas Aquinas was old enough to receive his first lessons, his parents—observing a custom that their rank and social class stipulated—confided their son to the care of Benedictine monks who dwelt about twenty kilometers south of Roccasecca at Montecassino. When Thomas arrived there in about 1230 or 1231, Montecassino, which was founded in the sixth century by Saint Benedict himself, had begun to enter a cycle of decline. Like the energies of individual Christian believers, the enthusiasms of corporate Christian bodies, dioceses, monasteries, etc., can wax and wane. Whether in good times or bad, however, this *Terra Sancti Benedicti* managed to remain a place of cultural and religious formation. Thomas, it is thought, came to the monastery as an oblate, that is, as someone who would remain within the claustral confines without, however, pronouncing religious vows. In all likelihood, it was at Montecassino that the young Thomas Aquinas first approached the Eucharist. Thomas the adolescent left Montecassino probably around 1239. At the same time, he never abandoned the Benedictine heritage, with its emphasis on the *magister*-disciple relationship that the monks had instilled in him during his formative years. From the ideals enshrined in the Rule of Saint Benedict, the lay oblate learned that one must practice humility in order to discover truth and to practice the other virtues. The German scholar Martin Grabmann has used three characteristics to describe the spiritual physiognomy of Thomas Aquinas: wisdom, charity, and peace.[16] These are the qualities of soul that medieval monasticism promoted and that it communicated to the new religious movements that began to flourish in the thirteenth century.

When Aquinas came to compose his *Summa theologiae*, he placed wisdom, charity, and peace at the pinnacle of the Christian moral life.[17] One may describe being wise as the state of the person who follows the theological or theologal path. The *Catechism of the Catholic Church* calls the prayer of Jesus to the Father "the theologal path (the path of faith, hope, and charity)."[18] In sum, the wise person is the one who lives a godly life. Those who possess charity, therefore, eschew ungodly habits: hatred, spiritual apathy, and envy. They also shun discord, contentiousness, and schism. They further avoid war, brawling, sedition, and scandal (which can kill the soul of another). This means that those who live a charity-infused life create around them what the Christian tradition calls the tranquility of order. Saints Augustine and Thomas Aquinas both adopt this definition of peace.[19]

A later spiritual author who was familiar with Aquinas's works identifies five effects of charity that appear in that person who follows the theologal path with its culmination in charity. First, says Saint John of the Cross, charity establishes a mutual friendship between the human person and Almighty God. This friendship may be described as a sending of the Holy Spirit that enables us to sustain a reciprocal love for God. Saint Paul made this point when he wrote that "the love of God has been poured out into our hearts through the holy Spirit that has been given to us" (Rom 5:5). This outpouring entails a mutual relatedness that really exists between the intelligent creature and God. Second, the charitable person rejoices in the flourishing of God's work. One might say that this quality describes the person who prays the Our Father with sincerity of heart. Each petition of this prayer expresses the desire that God govern his creation and cause it to flourish according to his will. Third, the person who loves God above all things acquires a knowledge of creatures and of their orderly arrangement in the universe. In other words, they do not prefer creatures to the love of God, but love creatures within the parameters of the natural and divine moral law. In order to love rightly, one must judge wisely. Fourth, our loving God above all things opens up to a loving gaze upon the divine. The person who loves God also contemplates God in Himself. Contemplation, as explained above, marks the highest activity in which the Christian engages. Fifth, charity and contemplation, the sanctification of heart and mind, result in a transformation of the whole person. To sum up, the term of the theologal life or path arrives at our total transformation in charity.[20] In other words, we become saints. For his part, Aquinas would come to prize those who managed to maintain a harmony between the performing of charitable deeds and the practice of contemplative prayer.[21]

In the Benedictine monks who were his teachers and his first spiritual guides, the young Thomas Aquinas first witnessed the transformative power of divine charity. He again learned early on that growth in charity means the cutting away of bad habits that oppose the tranquility of order. The lesson is simple to summarize: charity purifies us. To cite again Saint John of the Cross: "Although the flame in this life is very perfect and consummating in love, it is still also somewhat consuming and destructive, acting as fire does on coal; although coal is conformed with and transformed into the fire, and does not fume as it did before the transformation, still the flame that consummated the coal in fire consumed and reduced it to ashes."[22] The fire and ashes metaphor, of course, points to a person's purification that unfolds throughout his life and prepares that wayfarer for beholding the beatific vision. One may consider this vivid quotation a poetic transposition of a teaching that receives a less metaphorical expression in Aquinas's own writings.[23] The consuming transformation begins at Baptism and progresses (in patterns that differ from individual to individual) throughout the Christian's life. As we will recount later, this transformative process began in Aquinas from his earliest years and reached a certain symbolic conclusion at the end of his life.

Charity stands at the center and summit of the Christian life. Wisdom recapitulates the whole of instruction on the Christian life. So it is helpful to realize that for the perfection of the human person there exists no other lifestyle than what charity ordains: secular humanism leaves the natural desire for God unfulfilled; those who claim they are spiritual but not religious create for themselves an illusion in which to dwell; the agnostic makes a vain effort to hedge his bet. The only alternative to a life of charity is to return to idols, of one kind or another, as Saint Paul points out to the converts at Thessalonika (see 1 Thes 1:5–10). This explains why Wisdom is the only gift of the Holy Spirit that Aquinas in his schema of virtues, gifts, and beatitudes matches with a description of an anti-gift, so to speak, which he calls Folly (*stultitia*). What is characteristic of the foolish man? Aquinas describes it aptly: he plunges "his mind in earthly things, thereby making it incapable of perceiving the divine."[24] One may observe that never, or almost never, does one encounter a chaste fool.

The tenacity exhibited by the baby Thomas Aquinas, when he would not surrender the paper on which the words "Ave Maria" were written, foretold the wholehearted attachment that, once having achieved his maturity, he demonstrated unwaveringly toward God and the things of God. Later, he would describe Wisdom as a gift of the Holy Spirit that enables the believer to act because of a felt sympathy with God. The wise person clings tenaciously, if you will, to God, and so develops a sensitivity to the things of God. Wisdom, charity's gift, judges aright through a certain connaturality or sympathy with divine things.[25] We therefore rightly expect to find in such a wise person a model of virtuous living.

Though philosophers look for wisdom, Christians follow the theologian's quest. Christian wisdom recognizes indubitably that God remains, without qualification, the highest cause, and so this gift of the Holy Spirit comes down "from above," as the Letter of James puts it: "But the wisdom from above is first of all pure. Then peaceable, gentle, compliant, full of mercy and good fruits" (Jas 3:17). *Tranquillus Deus tranquillat omnia.* The tranquil God soothes all things. Thus the seventh beatitude finds congruence between charity and wisdom: "Blessed are the peacemakers for they shall be called children of God" (Mt 5:9). "Charity means having peace," writes Aquinas, "but bringing peace about belongs to ordering wisdom. And the Holy Spirit is called the Spirit of adoption because we receive from him the likeness of the natural Son who is Wisdom Begotten."[26] No wonder the man from Roccasecca devoted his whole life to an accurate presentation of the doctrine of Christian salvation. He discovered early on that those who embrace the truth also come to experience the sanctifying power of that truth in their lives. In other words, they become wise, that is, they enjoy a personal possession of the Highest Truth that governs all things.

THE BOND OF CHASTITY

And then, while he slept,
two angels came to tell him
that God had heard his prayer.
Then they bound his loins so tightly
that he felt the pain of it, saying to him:
"In God's name we bind you,
as you have asked to be bound,
with the bond of chastity that never shall be loosened."

Gui, "Life," 7

The Order of Preachers, or the Dominicans, came into existence as the result of an encounter between a fiery Castillian priest and an intractable Christian heresy. This providential meeting occurred in the area of southern France around Toulouse. The priest, Dominic Guzman, died in 1221, five years after Pope Honorius III (1148–1227), in December of 1216, had confirmed the Order of Preachers as an authentic form of Catholic religious life. The Dominican Order spread quickly throughout Europe. By 1231 in Naples, Dominicans were working out of a church dedicated to Saint Michael the Archangel that Benedictine monks had given them. The Holy Roman Emperor Frederick II had established a university in Naples around the time of Aquinas's birth (1224), and Dominicans were drawn to places where centers of higher education flourished. There at the Naples priory, the collegian Thomas encountered in due course the Dominican friars.

Although the family of Saint Thomas had foreseen an ecclesiastical career for their junior son, the Aquino family's social standing indicated that he should receive a post of clerical prestige. When therefore family members learned that the young Thomas planned to join the newly established Dominicans, they reacted as if the order of their universe was about to be shaken. Every effort was made to deter Thomas from his embracing what, in the eyes of the Aquinos, would result in unrealized potential. It would be as if the son of an industrial baron had announced that he wanted to operate a vegetable pushcart. As a result of this understandable though purely human reaction, sometime during the beginning of the 1240s, Thomas found himself under what one might describe as a sort of benign house arrest, after being forcibly removed from the company of the Dominicans. His brothers, who planned the abduction, being soldierly and worldly in their outlooks, devised what seemed to them a harmless plan to distract the young prisoner. They procured a woman of easy virtue, "a lovely but shameless girl," and introduced her into his living quarters.[27]

Saints react differently from one another to such trials. Some holy men have been known to attempt the conversion of women sent to seduce them. Thomas, however, took another path; he withstood—insistently, it is said—the woman's allurements. This withstanding, which is clearly attested in the earliest accounts of the saint's life, includes a scene that shows Thomas brandishing a fiery torch at the poor woman, who, as one may surmise, promptly departed from his room. With the charred torch, Thomas then made the sign of the cross on the wall of his cell. Kneeling before this improvised icon of Christ's victory over sin, he prayed: "Through this cross, a most holy sign/ Flee from me, thou spirit malign."[28] The moral is clear. God strengthens virtue in those who seek it. Since the fourteenth century, Thomas has served as a patron for purity and chastity. For angels are said to have rewarded Thomas's virtue by girding him with a cord around his waist. Although the post-mortem title of "Angelic Doctor" probably derives from Aquinas's exquisite treatise on the angels, the French scholar Pierre Mandonnet affirms that Thomas was also angelic in the practice of virtue.[29] More poignant testimony comes from the

Dominican who preached at Thomas's funeral and who had been his confessor: "I have heard this holy man's general confession and I bear witness that he was as pure as a five-year's-old child; he never felt the corruption of the flesh."[30]

As the black and white habit of Saint Dominic that accompanies every depiction of Thomas Aquinas confirms, the objections of his family gave way to the power of the Holy Spirit. Thomas Aquinas began his work in the Church as one of the early members of a religious order that—in large measure thanks to Aquinas—has become recognized for its commitment to the preaching of sanctifying truth. After 800 years of corporate existence, the Dominicans today are hardly fly-by-night outsiders, but they were newcomers on the Neapolitan scene of the mid-thirteenth century. For his part, Thomas Aquinas must have recognized in these vigorous white-clad friars a commitment to the intellectual life that corresponded to the native gifts of intelligence that he himself possessed. Though his own people wanted a career for him that would solidify the family's position in their native region, God directed Thomas Aquinas to the frontiers of thirteenth-century ecclesiastical life. One must assume further that Thomas was drawn by the display of evangelical urgency that the Dominicans brought to Neapolitan Catholic life of his day. In the end, the Aquino family withdrew their opposition to Thomas's plan to enter the Dominicans. According to Tocco, Thomas was allowed to escape from confinement at the ancestral domains. Like Saint Paul, he was let down by a rope into the hands of his Dominican brethren, who returned him to their priory in Naples.[31] There, near the end of his life, Thomas Aquinas would receive a divine confirmation of his decision to eschew preferment for mendicancy.

The rise of the mendicant orders (so called because their members declined established benefices and other emoluments that older religious institutions had acquired over the centuries) introduced a new sort of enthusiasm into Western Christianity. Benedict loved the mountains; Bernard, the valleys; Francis, the towns; and Dominic, the cities. Benedictine monasticism and the reform of it undertaken in the early twelfth century by Bernard of Clairvaux suited the spiritual needs of feudal, agrarian Europe. Monks provided a still and stable point of charity and peace within a political and social order that had to contend with the vagaries of a developing Western civilization. Pope Saint Leo the Great's fifth-century meeting with the Hunnish leader Attila is an icon of this engagement of the

Church with forces of disorder. Some centuries later, the Europe of the High Middle Ages underwent cultural, economic, and political changes that required a new kind of evangelical outreach. Francis of Assisi and his numerous followers tended to the needs of the town dwellers, whereas Dominic Guzman and his preaching-teaching friars headed for the new social reality called the city, with its centers of education that were located outside of the monastery. To advance this work, God inspired the young man from Roccasecca.

When the young Thomas Aquinas joined the Dominicans, he chose a life of perpetual continence. Religious life aims to provide a structure within which members can approach a perfect imitation of Christ. Why does perpetual continence contribute to the imitation of Christ? The answer becomes clear when one reflects that Christ himself was not married. He instead comes among us as a virginal, chaste, and loving man.

Aquinas chooses in his writings to locate perpetual continence within the context of the vowed person's need to focus intently on God. When he asks the question whether perpetual continence is required for religious profession, Aquinas turns to the words of Saint Paul found in 1 Corinthians 7:34.[32] There, Saint Paul remarks on the differences between married and unmarried women: "An unmarried woman or a virgin is anxious about the things of the Lord, so that she may be holy in both body and spirit." In other words, Aquinas places his emphasis on the way that perpetual continence favors the development of a person's relationship with God. In particular, he says that since the vowed religious state of life orders a person toward a complete dedication to divine service, the consecrated person should forego those things which impede such dedication.[33] In keeping with opinions found in both Aristotle and Saint Augustine, Aquinas makes his own the view that "the use of sexual pleasure withdraws the soul from that perfect intention of tending to God."[34] This conclusion builds on the principle Aristotle sets down in his treatment of temperance, namely, that an "intensity of pleasure" causes a person to lose a sense of proportion about reality.[35]

This viewpoint is not the equivalent of affirming that the procurement of sexual pleasure always brings sin. Still less does Aquinas consider sexual pleasure an intrinsic evil. For example, in his consideration of the First Parents, Aquinas argues that sexual pleasure would have been exquisitely realized in their copulations—were they to have had them—because "the lower energies were completely subject to reason."[36] After original sin, however, that complete subjection to right reason suffers a certain disordering that can result in one's experiencing a disproportionate bout of concupiscence. Therein of course lies the distraction from God. Another consideration examines the difficulties that marriage and family can entail. Aquinas makes his own what Saint Paul says about the married man, "who is anxious about the things of the world, how he may please his wife" (1 Cor 7:33). Indeed, Saint Paul goes so far as to call the married man "divided" (1 Cor 7:34). Again, Aquinas does not depreciate family life. However, he recognizes that the attentions wife and children rightly require do inescapably reduce the time available to a man for service to the Church. Not to mention a husband's less perfect imitation of the unmarried Christ.

Aquinas considers chastity a virtue because he holds that the impulse emotions can be "moderated," that is, shaped by reason.[37] He further explains that virtuous reason points the person toward a proper conformity with the divine design. So reason does not check emotion, but rather, as happens in any virtue, right reason conforms our capacities to some authentic good of the human person. In other words, virtue puts reason into emotion so that the person embraces promptly, joyfully, and easily those true goods of the human person that perfect him or her. Significantly, Aquinas also recognizes a metaphorical meaning for chastity that touches directly on divine charity and, thereby, the principal commandment of the Law, which forbids placing any creature or created thing before God. In the end, all unchastity becomes a form of idolatry.

In order to understand Aquinas's teaching about the restraining power of chastity, one has to distinguish between an intermission of reason that leaves human intelligence in a state of suspension and one that leads to a disordering of the mind's reasoning powers. Virtuous sex falls into the first category, whereas undue intoxication provides an example of the latter. Just as the Church teaches today that communication in charity enhances the fun of marriage, so in Aquinas there is nothing that would allow one to conclude that sex makes one behave more like animals except the honest realization that disordered sex does mar the beauty of the creature in a way that other capital sins do not, "for a person sunk in carnal delights has no taste for spiritual joys."[38] In the end, Aquinas puts a positive interpretation onto chastity, namely, that chastity purifies a person in order that he or she can sustain the contemplation of divine truths.[39] It follows that Aquinas would further consider all disordered or disproportionate movements of sexual emotion as moving the person away from what is "most excellently beautiful."[40]

One may conclude from what Aquinas teaches about chastity that the vice of lust in any of its forms weakens the believer's spiritual clinging to Jesus and Mary. The temptation to make exceptions in the matters of chastity risks grave spiritual harm for the baptized person and places in jeopardy his or her commitment to live as a new creation. There are, of course, many cultural factors that do affect the culpability of the unchaste person, but even when such factors result in decreased culpability, the unchaste thought, word, or deed still leaves the person debilitated with respect to achieving a full life of loving communion with God and the neighbor.

The Angelic Warfare Confraternity continues to promote Aquinas's love for the virtue of chastity. The Angelic Doctor learned early on about the importance of a chaste life for every member of the Church. In a word, the chaste person makes the best lover. This rule applies to those in consecrated or religious life as well as to those in the married state. Those who join this Confraternity receive a white cord similar to the one with which the angels girded Aquinas. Worn around the waist, the blessed cord reminds the wearer that one's vocation within the Church, cleric, consecrated, or lay, reaches its best realization when wrongly procured sexual pleasure no longer mars the person's love for God.

HIS HEART WAS
GROUNDED IN HUMILITY

And the story goes that at last Albert exclaimed:
"We call this lad a dumb ox,
but I tell you that the whole world
is going to hear his bellowing!"
Such praise would breed conceit in most young men,
but on Thomas it had no such effect,
for his heart was grounded in humility.

Gui, "Life," 10

Thomas's return to the Dominicans caused great joy among his brethren. However, they took no chances that his blood family might change their minds and come to fetch Thomas and bring him back to their care and their plans for his future. Almost immediately, Thomas Aquinas found himself heading back up the Italian peninsula from Naples (which during much of the second millennium was considered part of the Kingdom of the Two Sicilies), traveling toward Rome. There he met the Master of the Dominican Order, John the Teuton, who arranged that the young and gifted student would be sent to Cologne on the Rhine. Once arrived, Thomas met Master Albert (d. 1280), a German Dominican renowned for his universal learning and who even in his lifetime was called "the Great." Between 1248 and 1252, Thomas joined other young Dominicans from around Europe who learned from this teacher of excellence about the things of God and his creation. In all likelihood, Thomas Aquinas received priestly ordination while he lived and studied in Cologne. It was also during the Cologne period that Thomas was dubbed the "dumb ox from Sicily." The good-natured nickname reflects the fact that Thomas Aquinas was both corpulent of stature and taciturn of spirit. Albert the Great, as Bernard Gui reports, acknowledged that Thomas was called the Sicilian Ox, and he also predicted, as already mentioned, that the bellows of this ox would reach around "the whole world."

It is generally agreed that Master Albert exercised an intellectual influence on the young Thomas Aquinas. One prominent biographer of Aquinas, Jean-Pierre Torrell, o.p., concludes that Thomas served as an assistant to the Cologne master and that, like assistants of today's university professors, Thomas was given certain teaching responsibilities.[41] Some of Aquinas's writings on the Sacred Scriptures, especially on the Old Testament, may find their origin in the "cursory," expositive instruction that Thomas gave to students at the Cologne general study house. From his empirically minded German teacher (who is credited with the discovery of arsenic), Thomas also discovered the confidence that the theologian should place in created things. He came to recognize the things of creation as expressions of the divine wisdom, much as the talent of the artist can be discerned in an artwork.

During his stay in Cologne, Thomas Aquinas was shaped in his personal development by the form of life that he lived with others in community. The Dominican ideal requires that a man give himself over to prayer, common life, study, and the profession of the evangelical counsels, which for Dominicans is expressed in the single promise of obedience. Dominican prayer finds its eminent expression in the common celebration of the choral office and at the celebration of Mass. Thomas Aquinas prized this practice of common prayer. Consider his reaction to the Latin antiphon *Media vita in morte sumus*, which was (and still is) sung by Dominicans during Lent. The biographers of Aquinas report that when he heard this antiphon in chapel, Brother Thomas was moved to tears of supplication.[42] Being a Dominican was not, for Thomas Aquinas, a matter of his maintaining school loyalties or choosing a lifestyle to suit his academic career. Dominican life suited his thirst for holiness. Both prayer and study, each in its own way a contemplative activity, develop out of the Christian assent to faith. When Aquinas was moved to assent to the truths that the Church proposed for belief, he found himself also directed toward prayerful worship of the Truth. When he pondered the truths that God has revealed, Aquinas's pursuit of theological excellence moved him to embrace the Truth that he studied. Since prayer and study both unite a believer with the mysteries by which the Highest Truth makes himself known, they complement one another in that gift of the Holy Spirit called Wisdom. As I have said above, this highest of the Holy Spirit's gifts penetrates both mind and will. Those who possess this gift of grace exhibit in a most excellent way the sanctifying power of divine Truth.

It is easy to overlook the fact that Thomas Aquinas accomplished his massive literary output within the highly structured rhythms of a common life. Dominican conventual life entails common meals, shared recreation, and choral prayer lived out within an architectural structure specifically designed to accommodate these activities. Dominican life requires a form that is visible. One of the best surviving structures that illustrates this Dominican style of architecture stands in Toulouse at L'Église des Jacobins where, as mentioned above, the relics of Saint Thomas Aquinas have found their final resting place. Chapel for prayer; refectory for meals; library and cells for study; chapter room to conduct the daily governance of the community. Each element of Dominican life contributes to the knitting together of the composite form. The extraordinary literary output we call his works was sustained through his participation in the daily rhythms of Dominican life.

Because of the scientific model that Aquinas and the scholastics used to develop their theological arguments, some modern readers may come away with the impression that Aquinas constructs his theology, as it were, out of whole cloth. True enough, precision was the tool of the medieval schoolmen's theological trade. A thinker like Aquinas, however, distinguishes himself by the attention that he pays to the sources of theology. The Toronto scholar James A. Weisheipl, O.P., relates a story (which appears in Guillaume de Tocco's 1323 *Ystoria sancti Thome de Aquino*) that captures the nature of Aquinas's intellectual curiosity. Once when he (then a teacher) and some students were returning to Paris from the countryside, one of his companions said to Thomas, "Look, Master, what a fine city Paris is! Wouldn't you like to be the lord of it?" Thomas answered, "What would I do with it?" Not taking the hint, the student replied to Thomas, "You could sell it to the king of France and use all the money to build all the places for the Dominican Friars." "I would rather," replied Thomas, "have the homilies of Chrysostom on the Gospel of Saint Matthew."[43]

This incident discloses Aquinas's humble appreciation for the authoritative sources that contribute to one's understanding of the Catholic faith. Saint Thomas understood *ressourcement* in the deepest sense of that term. His reverence for authority flowed not from a curiosity about how different views dialectically influence the development of this or that topic within a certain discipline. He appreciated rather the place that recognized teachers hold in the communication of Catholic doctrine. Thomas Aquinas surely did not harbor the ambition of showing that he knew more than anyone else about authors in a field of study. He instead sought the best authorities. Because of their capacity to make a person wise, Thomas Aquinas revered sound theological opinions. In a homily that he preached before the teachers and students at Paris, Aquinas asks, "Where ought we to seek wisdom and from whom?" He continues, addressing the young students, "You should not be satisfied inquiring only of the ones [masters] who are present, but you ought to inquire also of the old ones who are not with us anymore. If you do not have an abundance of people, you still have an abundance of texts. When you see texts of Augustine and Ambrose, examine these."[44] By the thirteenth century, Montecassino had built up one of the best collections of books in Europe. Early on, then, Thomas Aquinas learned how to appreciate the importance of a library as a place to make new friends. Because the acquisition of divine truth sanctifies, libraries also merit recognition for their silent contribution to growth in holiness.

Saint Thomas devotes an article in his *Summa theologiae* to whether the moral virtues play a role in the contemplative life. One must hold two truths together in a certain tension. On the one hand, holiness of life becomes the contemplative, whereas moral virtue and contemplation each achieve different objectives in the perfection of the human person. So Aquinas says bluntly: The moral virtues do not directly and alone produce contemplation, "because the goal of the contemplative life is the consideration of truth."[45] Still, the consideration of divine truth does stand at the heart of Aquinas's conception of the moral life. This means that the moral virtues, which shape the behavior of a person in conformity with the imperatives of right reason, do contribute to the well-being of the Christian believer who seeks to maintain a steady beholding of truth. In Aquinas's phrase, the fruitful possession of the moral virtues disposes the virtuous man or woman to engage in the high demands of contemplation. Aquinas goes on to explain why such a disposing proves indispensable for contemplation. "The act of contemplation," he says, "in which the contemplative life consists essentially, is impeded by the vehemence of the passions, which turn the soul's desire from things of mind to things of sense, and by external disturbances."[46] The moral virtues, prudence, justice, fortitude, and temperance, each in its distinctive fashion, restrain passion and quell (as much as possible) external disturbances. What is true of those who cultivate a strictly contemplative life applies as well to all Christians who wish to maintain a steadiness in their everyday pursuit of holiness.

Examples come easily. Consider the moral virtue of prudence. Constancy holds a central place in the unfolding of prudence's role of guiding human behavior according to right reason. In fact, inconstancy works against prudence, inasmuch as this vice turns the prudent man into a wavering shirker in the execution of a good deed.[47] It becomes difficult to imagine how an inconstant person would discover the energies to remain steadfast in the pursuit of contemplation or of any other sanctifying good.

Next, consider justice. In a word, the man who fails to give others their due, which describes the unjust person, will hardly find the resolve to give God the due mental attention that contemplation requires, and so may fall short in carrying out all the obligations of a virtuous life. Unjust persons, thieves and robbers, liars and calumniators, in fact find themselves viciously occupied with external disturbances of their own making.

The moral virtues of fortitude and temperance provide further examples of the place of the moral virtues in the maintenance of a contemplative outlook on life. Contemplation does not become the pusillanimous, for the fault of pusillanimity, a vice opposed to fortitude, withdraws one from high aims rather than urging their pursuit.[48] Regarding temperance: Aquinas, as we have seen, follows the dominant Christian tradition that locates the greatest opposition to contemplation in the vice of lust, for contemplation readies a person to behold the beauty that surrounds the Christian mysteries. Sordidness, by contrast, obscures beauty.

Within this context, one can fruitfully measure the usefulness of social media and the vast empire of internet resources. Reasonable use of the internet has become a feature of everyday life. Some options no longer exist. For example, airline offices, where once upon a time the traveler could speak to an agent about bookings, today find their replacement in an impersonal Internet app. At the same time, the internet roams, like the devil, prowling for souls to devour. Much of what distracts, to be sure, falls under the heading of lust. The internet, though, also poses many temptations against the virtue of study, especially in the many opportunities to indulge the vice of *curiositas*. Aquinas points out that curiosity concerns not so much knowing as hankering to find out, and he lists four ways in which curiosity can corrupt a person.[49] All should agree, however, that no one can sustain a contemplative life, that is, the pondering of sanctifying truth, without exercising great moderation and even caution with respect to use of the internet.

Among the moral virtues that best prepare a person to discover truth and to ponder it fruitfully (activities that stand at the heart of contemplation), humility occupies a special place. Aquinas, a man of prodigious intellectual ability, demonstrates the humility that one would expect to discover in a saint without much learning. Paris meant nothing, but the homilies of a great Church Father would meet his needs. No wonder he describes humility within the context of one's seeking difficult but good things. Humility, writes Aquinas, tempers and restrains the mind lest it press forward immoderately to high things.[50] Note how Aquinas's view of humility does not correspond to the self-deprecating attitudes that some later spiritual authors have suggested to their readers. Aquinas's humble man is no Roger Milquetoast. Instead, the humble person knows which goods will suit his pursuit of holiness and pursues them moderately but also resolutely. Aquinas, in fact, considers the virtue of humility in the same context within which he discusses magnanimity, the Christian virtue that bolsters a person to undertake and to complete great things, again in accordance with right reason.

Spiritual authors including Aquinas indicate the indispensable place that humility holds in the pursuit of sanctity. This notion finds early authentication in the seventh chapter of the *Rule of Saint Benedict*. Humility checks Pelagian impulses whereby we try to save ourselves; at the same time, this virtue establishes us in a right dependency on the divine will. This explains why the Blessed Virgin Mary stands out as a model of humility, especially at the central moment of her life, the Annunciation: "May it be done to me according to your word" (Lk 1:38). No wonder Aquinas concludes that "humility implies most of all man's subjection to God."[51]

TO RISE
INTO SPECULATION

⁂

Here too we may touch on Thomas's habit of reading
from time to time in one of those collections
of *Homilies of the Fathers*, which he did
in order to offset the aridity
which is so often the result of abstract
and subtle speculative thinking.
He himself used to say that after a spell
of this sort of reading
he found it easier to rise into speculation,
so that it did both his heart good by increasing devotion,
and his intellect by deepening its considerations.
Gui, "Life," 16

The university at Paris was among the first places in Europe where scholars and students came
together to pursue advanced studies. By the time
Thomas Aquinas was sent there, certain official
recognitions had given the university a structure.
At the same time, as a major center of learning
for Christendom, Paris had already experienced a
long and turbulent university history. Strikes were
a commonplace. Thomas came to Paris with the
strong support of Albert the Great, who better
than anyone recognized his assistant's intellectual prowess. Extensive research about the medieval
universities and the practices that developed within

them provides us with a fairly clear picture of the manner in which Thomas Aquinas was introduced into the Parisian model. Junior theology professors were required to demonstrate their competence in treating two key texts that were considered normative for Christian theology. As a first step, the aspiring professor had to show that he was familiar with the texts of the canonical scriptures. The biblical bachelor had to make sense out of the Bible. During certain periods of the Christian centuries and in many places throughout the Christian world, clerics were satisfied to know snippets of the Bible. What they needed for preaching, for giving catechetical instruction, and for providing moral guidance and encouragement sufficed. The urbanization of Europe produced a heightened awareness of the need for a better-educated clergy. Careful and complete reading of the biblical texts ensured that the cleric in formation would at least have heard all of sacred scripture. It is assumed that Aquinas completed this prefatory phase of his advanced theological formation, which would be the equivalent of today's graduate school qualification exams, in Cologne.

Once the aspiring professor of theology had shown his competence in the sacred texts, he was required to demonstrate his capacity for dealing with the Tradition and the Magisterium. The Bible contains divine revelation. Holy Tradition and the Magisterium of the Church complete the presentation of divine truth that God has confided to the Church for the salvation of souls. As a result of the developments in theological education that began in the early twelfth century, a period of renaissance not only for theology but also for the human sciences, the givens of the faith were organized into systematic presentations that would compare favorably with the modern-day textbook. These organized collections of authentic Catholic teachings gave a pedagogical structure to the teaching of theology. The book that became the model for theological instruction throughout Western Europe is the work of a twelfth-century cleric named Peter the Lombard. *The Four Books of the Sentences* supplied to generations of Christian thinkers a context for theological discussion. Even after the *Summa theologiae* of Aquinas had replaced the *Sentences* as the basis for classroom instruction, commentaries on the Lombard's work were studied, well into the modern period. Thomas Aquinas had not completed his own commentary on the Lombard's *Sentences* when in 1256 he was admitted to the ranks of the university masters. As a *magister*, Thomas was entitled to resolve questions that arose in the course of the disputations whereby the schoolmen hammered out their differences. During the thirteenth century at Paris, many masters resolved questions. Most of their resolutions have been forgotten. What is unique about Thomas Aquinas is the fact that a large number of his conclusions not only have survived but also have shaped the official teachings of the Catholic Church. Thomas Aquinas enjoys a currency today that other medieval masters like Henry of Ghent, Godfrey of Fontaines, or Peter of Tarrentaise, who was known in his day as *famosissimus doctor*, do not.

Thomas lived at the Dominican priory in Paris, which was located near where today begins the Rue Soufflot, the street that, in the heart of Paris, runs down from the Pantheon. In addition to his class preparations and writings, Thomas gave himself over to the activities of a medieval master: *legere, disputare,* and *praedicare*—to read, to dispute, to preach. He "read" or commented on the Bible; he disputed, that is, he resolved questions of the day; he preached. The university sermons of Thomas Aquinas only lately have been made widely available. The sermons complement what we know of Aquinas from his more famous works, especially his *summae*. They also provide glimpses into Aquinas's personal views that otherwise may escape notice.

For example, we learn the important value that he placed on spiritual generation. In the aforementioned sermon where he instructs the students to revere the works of dead masters, Aquinas also directs those who seek wisdom to find a living teacher. First of all, he proclaims, seek wisdom "from a *magister* or from people who are wiser [than you are]. Hence it says in Deuteronomy 32:7: 'Ask your father,' that is, a *magister*. Because, as a father has brought you forth physically, a *magister* brings you forth spiritually."[52] The parallel is instructive: just as the father begets a child who grows up to generate others, so the teacher of sacred doctrine begets children in the faith who are capable of instructing others. Authentic masters of the Christian religion do not undertake an ideological campaign to indoctrinate others. Clonal reproduction is not their trade. Masters liberate others from the darkness of ignorance so that these persons can use their own intelligence to, in a word, become saints.

The mendicant friars of course were newcomers to the Parisian scene of the mid-thirteenth century. Not all the establishment figures welcomed them with open arms. Indeed it well may have happened that Thomas Aquinas was sent to Paris to assist the mendicants in their efforts to rebut the specious "theological" arguments that self-serving secular clerics had developed in an effort to protect their privileges. The so-called anti-mendicant controversy revealed that the wise, charitable, peaceful, and humble Thomas Aquinas was also quite capable of putting up a good fight when the circumstances, and charity itself, warranted it. He did not, for instance, fear to denounce the clandestine methods of those who tried to dissuade young men from joining the Dominicans. "Let them not go and babble to children," he cried out, but they should instead write a book and publish it so that their views might be judged by "the authority of the truth."[53] These words reveal the spiritual temper of Aquinas, a man who displays his mettle by his commitment to and deep trust in "the authority of the truth."

In order to provide well-trained teachers for the other places where the Dominican Order took root, thirteenth-century Dominican policy arranged for a quick rotation of masters at Paris. When he finished his term, Thomas Aquinas returned to Italy, and the English Dominican William of Alton took over from him. For his part, Thomas Aquinas continued his service to the truth by teaching, writing, and providing learned counsel to ecclesiastical authorities. Although he visited several Italian cities, we know that Thomas resided at Dominican priories in Orvieto (1261–65), Rome (1265–68), and, perhaps, back in Naples. The medieval popes moved around their temporal domains, just as the secular rulers of the time moved their courts. Pope Urban IV (1261–64) kept court at Orvieto, another Italian hill town. One biographer of Aquinas, Tolomeo of Lucca, explains: "When, for definite reasons, Brother Thomas had to be recalled from Paris, he did a great deal of literary work for Pope Urban."[54] We now possess, thanks to the use Pope Urban made of Friar Thomas d'Aquino, the liturgical texts for the feast of Corpus Christi, especially the Sequence *Lauda Sion*.[55] It is impossible to separate Aquinas's speculative achievements from his service to the teaching ministry of the Catholic Church. The modern secular university would have been as foreign to Thomas Aquinas as a vegetable pushcart to the son of an industrial baron.

What is the truth that sanctifies? This truth finds concrete expression in the articles of Christian faith. These articles take the form of propositions of faith, such as one finds in the Apostles' Creed, for example, "I believe in God, [who is] the Father almighty." These sentences make truth claims about objective realities. When he inquires how an article of faith sanctifies the one who professes it, Aquinas includes in his reply elements of both the reality and the proposition. Aquinas recognizes that the articles of faith both contain a divine reality and can be formulated in sentences.

How does Aquinas come to recognize the article of faith as more than a mere formula on which adherents of the Catholic faith agree? How does he come to recognize that the articles of faith as they appear in the Christian creeds are capable of uniting the believer to the very divine reality, the very Christian mystery that the article affirms? Aquinas's definition for an article materially depends on its Greek etymology, that is, "joint," as in the English word "arthritis." However, he deepens this first suggestion with a more developed account that describes an organic interdependence which, so to speak, is written into the heart of the article. According to this account, one must relate the articles of faith to the broader range of matters that the Church proposes for belief, such as, Christ is born of the Virgin Mary, suffers under Pontius Pilate, and will come again in glory. In fact, Aquinas develops an analogy along the lines of Aristotelian science. In this analogy, the operative model relates the principal articles, for example, Christ is born of the Virgin Mary, to the secondary articles, for example, Mary is Mother of the Church, and other things to be believed, for example, Mary enjoys a primacy of mediation in the bestowal of divine gifts and graces. Aquinas surely has in mind the way that *per se nota* principles, that is, principles for which there exist no prior arguments, stand in relation to conclusions in a teaching which natural reason elaborates.[56] To put it differently, the Creed that we recite every Sunday represents a recognizable body of saving truths to which Catholics assent. This assent of salvific faith carries with it the graces necessary to live in accord with all that the Church holds and teaches.

From God and the blessed to the angels to the prophets to Christ and his apostles to the prelates and teachers and preachers of the Church, Aquinas claims a real community in those who are taught and one universal causal order of principal to instrumental or ministerial teachers. Of course, on account of the Incarnation, in which God becomes man, Christ himself stands at the center of this entire process; it is he who teaches the angels. Aquinas subordinates the articles of faith to God, who as First Truth energizes them with saving power.[57]

This means that when the believer professes the articles of faith, he or she adheres to God himself, First Truth in Being and Speaking.

What is most important to remember, Aquinas's teaching explains that the act of faith reaches beyond the expression of doctrines and brings the believer into contact with God himself. This strong account of Christian doctrine develops partly as a result of Aquinas's view that belief constitutes a sort of theological judgment about reality.[58] In the celebrated phrase of Aquinas: Faith stops not at words but at reality.[59] For example, because the universal Church confesses the doctrine of the Immaculate Conception, each of the faithful believes that Mary is immaculately conceived. Accordingly, this article of faith—as set forth in Pius IX's *Ineffabilis Deus*, in this example—serves as an instrument for an action that surpasses the mere formulation of a dogma. Christian faith's judgment transcends the conceptual content of the proposition, the sentence, and it lays hold of the very realities that the articles express and mediate.[60] In the case of the Immaculate Conception, for example, the believer enters into the reality of Mary's spiritual motherhood and her existing as the first person to have benefitted from the salvation wrought by her Son.

Indeed, this penetration of the mystery can happen only because the dynamic of faith itself includes an affective component. Unlike ordinary knowing, which depends on sense contact with the object known, a person can accept the articles of faith as true only upon a personal surrender to the one God, who both exists as Truth and speaks the Truth. The volitional union of the believer with that which is believed subsequently begets an even greater love of the revealed truth. From this perspective, Aquinas easily affirms a continuity between living by faith here below and seeing by vision in heaven. This coherence, which grounds any development of dogma in the Church, depends upon that special outpouring of divine love that results in the Incarnation of the Word.

The intelligible character of the articles of faith lies at the heart of Aquinas's account of sanctifying truth. The articles have the capacity to unite us to the very mystery which the statement of the article enunciates. Indeed, the Catholic believer requires a form of contact with the saving reality that makes one holy, and the capacity of the human intellect to make that contact proves indispensable to the Christian religion. Otherwise, doctrines would serve only a social function, for example, to provide coherence and identity for a given community. The act of coming together, though, does not in itself sanctify. Statements, even creedal statements, do not sanctify. Only God sanctifies. Obviously the profession of faith that leads to a penetration or embrace of a Christian mystery requires various gifts and graces. Knowledge and Understanding, two gifts of the Holy Spirit, assist the believer to lay hold of such divine mysteries as the Nativity, the Crucifixion, the Church, Everlasting Life. In short, the believer is invited to make of the profession of faith a prayer of union between himself and the divine mystery confessed. At the same time, without a coherent account about how human knowing can attain the real, the believer is left to approach the articles of faith in terms of metaphor, narrative, and experience. Such categories, however, cannot assure contact with the real, especially with real truths that contain, as it were, the ultimately real, that is, that attain to God himself. No wonder Saint Thomas devoted so much energy to his study and his teaching. He knew well that his salvation and the salvation of others depend on getting things straight, that is, on attaining to truth about God. In this exercise, the Angelic Doctor lived up to his Dominican vocation. Indeed, in Saint Dominic's own vision, the purpose of the Order was to procure the salvation of its members as well as of others.[61] These happy outcomes occur most frequently when the teacher or the evangelist not only increases devotion in his hearers but also deepens their understanding or grasp of the articles of faith.

RUNNING STRONGLY
TO MEET HIS LORD

Feeling his strength ebbing away,
he devoutly asked for the most holy body of Christ;
and when the abbot, accompanied by the monks,
brought it to him, he did reverence to it,
prostrate on the ground;
weak in body, but with his mind, as it were,
running strongly to meet his Lord.

Gui, "Life," 39

Aquinas rarely discloses memorable details of his own personal life. How different do we find his literary style from that of Saint Augustine! There were, as already mentioned, the occasional scholastic scrapes that remain endemic to university life and which caused in him a few emotional sparks to fly. Then we have, in the epigraph just above, testimony to Aquinas's simplicity of spirit, a foundational disposition for anyone's acquiring the other virtues of the Christian life.

Thomas Aquinas was not inclined to seek the limelight. Once, for example, when our saint was staying at the Dominican house in Bologna, another friar summoned Aquinas to accompany him on a trip to the city. How could this happen, one may ask? In short, a companion was required for all movement outside the priory. The ancient Rule of Saint Augustine that Saint Dominic chose for his Order stipulates this provision.[62] So the prior (or superior) told the friar who was about to depart for Bologna to take with him as a companion the first person he encountered. Unbeknownst to this city-bound friar, that Dominican would turn out to be one Thomas Aquinas.

Bernard Gui's life of Saint Thomas Aquinas (excerpts from this "Life" have been placed at the head of each chapter) tells us what happened next: "Thomas bowed his head at once and followed. Now the other was a fast walker, too fast for Thomas, who could not keep up with him and got many hard words in consequence, but each time begged the other's pardon." Perhaps you can imagine the sight of these two Dominicans traversing downtown Bologna, a city where, so we discover, Aquinas had become well known to the local inhabitants. Gui continues: "And this was noticed and wondered at by the people in the city: for they recognized the great teacher who was hurrying after that undistinguished friar; and, thinking there must be some mistake, they at last told the latter who his companion was." The efficient though inconsiderate Dominican expressed his remorse, whereas Aquinas explained to the townsfolk that the path to perfection lies in obedience and humility, the virtues of Christ. So Bernard Gui, Saint Thomas's biographer, concludes: "O happily humble soul, you did not stand on your dignity…as an excuse for not obeying the prior through his spokesman. Though the habit of meditation made you a slow mover in the market-place, you were speedy enough in obedience—obedience the teacher of all virtues when joined to humility."[63] It is difficult to imagine a more touching account of the saint's personal composure. Even those who do not profess a vow of obedience to a superior can learn from this lesson Aquinas teaches, for example when they practice the obedience of faith. The *Catechism of the Catholic Church* puts it this way: "To obey…in faith is to submit freely to the word that has been heard, because its truth is guaranteed by God, who is Truth itself."[64]

As the above incident suggests, Saint Thomas's daily routine followed for the most part the predictable rhythms that belong to a Dominican priory and the university classroom. One must wait until the end of his life, when it is reported that Christ spoke to him from a crucifix, to discover something of the supernaturally fascinating associated with the life and experiences of Brother Thomas Aquinas.

The needs of the Dominicans at Paris required of Thomas Aquinas a second stint of teaching there (1268–72). In a word, competing theological paradigms had begun to develop among Catholic theologians. The introduction of Aristotle into the West, as Aquinas's own work makes evident, opened up a new way of looking at the relationship between God and the world, faith and reason, grace and nature. It requires an accomplished master to sort out the difficulties that can arise. The Church herself assures us that "Thomas had the great merit of giving pride of place to the harmony which exists between faith and reason."[65] When this second Parisian regency had come to an end, Thomas returned to the place where he had first met the Dominicans.

In beautiful Naples, he continued his teaching and writing and preaching. It was at this time that the young Dominican student William of Tocco, another contemporary biographer, encountered Aquinas. Today the magnificent basilica of San Domenico Maggiore in Naples houses the crucifix that spoke to Aquinas. The basilica's present structure was begun sometime after Thomas's death in 1274. However, the chapel of Saint Nicholas that survives from the earlier building can be seen. In that spot, while he was saying Mass on 6 December

1273, Saint Nicholas Day, Thomas Aquinas underwent a profound transformation of soul. He stopped his writing, and he left works unfinished. When asked to explain the sudden change in his work habits, Thomas said that he now looked upon what he had written as so much straw. The best interpreters opine that Aquinas must have experienced for himself what he had always taught: the articles of faith are instruments of one's embracing personally the mysteries of faith. Words pass over to reality. Truth sanctifies. The tradition places on Thomas's lips the words "*Non nisi te, Domine.*" Nothing but you yourself, O Lord. Words that Thomas addressed to the Crucified One when He asked what reward Thomas desired for all the excellent things that he had written about his Lord. Union with Christ, the Incarnate Word, brings to perfection in each Christian believer the sanctifying power of divine Truth.

Early in 1274, Thomas Aquinas once again set out northward from Naples. Pope Gregory X had summoned him to a council in Lyons, which would seek to heal the ecclesiastical breach between Rome and Constantinople. The invitation confirms the esteem in which popes of his period held Thomas Aquinas. Along the road up the Italian peninsula, Thomas fell ill. After spending a few days at his sister's castle, he was transported to the Cistercian Abbey of Fossanova. There, having received the Holy Eucharist and the Sacrament of Holy Anointing, he died early on 7 March 1274.

An ancient liturgical hymn recalls this moment and the saint's accomplishments: "*Lauda mater ecclesia Thomae felicem exitum qui pervenit ad gaudia per verbi vitae meritum.*"[66] Praise, Mother Church, the happy ending of Thomas, who arrived at [heavenly] joys through the merits of the Word of Life. He was canonized by Pope John XXII in 1323.

Aquinas, at the end of his life, demonstrates the fruitfulness of his own intellectual account of contemplation, which he describes as the mind's beholding of the Highest Truth. "Contemplation," recall, "refers to a simple gaze upon a truth."[67] He gazed upon the Crucified One and passed over to the Eternal Word. "Contemplation," as one of Aquinas's commentators remarked, "remains an act of intelligence; however this act finds both its cause and its termination in love."[68] For the human person, nothing can be considered superior to this attachment to Truth itself.

To summarize what Aquinas teaches us about the sanctifying power of divine truth, recall three points. First, since Thomist contemplation remains an act of intelligence, no Christian who wishes to maintain a living faith can shun study in some form or another. Studies, both philosophical and theological, obviously prepare one for contemplation. At the same time, more informal and even modest engagements with texts serve to root the believer in the sanctifying power of truth. For example, the more that spouses study what the *Catechism of the Catholic Church* teaches about marriage, the more they should come to cherish the fidelity and fecundity that marriage requires. Note, however, that the study must be geared to contemplative ends, not to information gathering.

Second, Aquinas considers the detachment, that is, quiet solitude, necessary in order to create an atmosphere for contemplation. The Christian believer can make anywhere a place for contemplation, provided that he or she remains focused on the divine mysteries. Obviously, the different vocations in the Church, clerical, consecrated, and lay, make diverse arrangements to accommodate this detachment. Family life ordinarily does not afford the same institutional solitude one finds in a monastery.

Third, Aquinas fully expects that an encounter with the Highest Good will produce true spiritual joy. In order to recognize such joy, it helps to consider aesthetic pleasure and the joy that it brings. There one probably finds the closest human analogy to spiritual joy. Aesthetic joy arises through one's beholding the clarity, proportion, and integrity found in beautiful created things. Thomas of the Creator never lost his appreciation for the divine order inherent in creation. Still, he discovered throughout his life and experienced at the end of it that the most beautiful things surpass the capacity of our senses to grasp. Only the eyes of faith can lay hold of those truths that sanctify the world. The Christian believer should express gratitude for those moments when an embrace of divine things brings joy.

The burden of this short exposition of Aquinas, a sort of spiritual biography, has been to expose the secret of his sanctity. Of course, the secret does not belong only to Saint Thomas or even to his followers, Thomists. The secret appears as the message of the gospel, a message that anyone moved by God's prevenient, that is, preceding, grace can embrace. We do this each time we studiously ponder the saving truths that the Catholic Church both preserves and unfolds in her teachings, in her liturgy, and in the witness of her saints. Among the latter, Thomas Aquinas holds a special place. He provides the architectural plan for Christian living in his expositions of sanctifying truth.

NOTES

1. *Codex Iuris Canonici (CIC)*, no. 252.

2. See the Second Vatican Council's Dogmatic Constitution On Divine Revelation, *Dei Verbum*, no. 8: "The words of the holy fathers witness to the presence of this living tradition, whose wealth is poured into the practice and life of the believing and praying Church."

3. See "Address of His Holiness Benedict XVI to the Roman Curia Offering Them His Christmas Greetings," Thursday, 22 December 2005.

4. *Fides et ratio*, no. 44.

5. Josef Pieper, *The Silence of St. Thomas*, trans J. Murray & D. O'Connor (Chicago, IL: Henry Regnery Co., 1965), p. 32.

6. See Romanus Cessario, O.P., *A Short History of Thomism* (Washington, DC: The Catholic University of America Press, 2005).

7. "A Letter of the Faculty of Arts in the University of Paris to the General Chapter of the Order of Preachers at Lyons in 1274," as cited in Foster, *Biographical Documents*, p. 15.

8. Guy Bedouelle, *The Reform of Catholicism: 1480–1620*, trans. J. K. Farge (Toronto: Pontifical Institute of Mediaeval Studies, 2008), p. 136.

9. For further discussion, see Romanus Cessario, O.P., and Cajetan Cuddy, O.P., *Thomas and the Thomists: The Achievement of Thomas Aquinas and His Interpreters* (Minneapolis: Fortress Press, 2017).

10. See 1 Sm 2:3 and the Apostolic Constitution *Deus Scientiarum Dominus*, On universities and faculties of ecclesiastical schools, by Pope Pius XI (24 May 1931).

11. From Thomas Aquinas, "A Letter on the Method of Study," trans. Steve Perkins (2004), at *Corpus Scriptorum Latinorum*: http://www.forumromanum.org/literature/aquinas/stud_e.html.

12. For a review of the materials that defend Aquino itself as the birthplace of Saint Thomas, see Constantino Jadecola, *San Tommaso d'Aquino. Sintesi della vita* (Aquino: I Edizione, 2002), pp. 19ff.

13. P. Angelo Walz, o.p., *Luoghi di San Tommaso* (Rome: Herder, 1961), pp. 24–26.

14. Gugliemo di Tocco, "Hystoria beati Thomae de Aquino" in S. Thomas Aquinatis *Vitae Fontes Praecipuae*, ed. Angelico Ferrua, o.p. (Alba: Edizioni Domenicane, 1968), pp. 25–123, no. 2.

15. Tocco, "Hystoria," pp. 32–34, no. 4.

16. Martin Grabmann, *Thomas Aquinas. His Personality and Thought* [1928], trans. Virgil Michel (New York: Russell & Russell, 1963).

17. See *Summa theologiae* II-II q. 45 on the gift of wisdom, which completes the treatise on the theological virtue of charity. Article six points out that the seventh Beatitude, "Blessed are the peacemakers" (Mt 5:9), corresponds to the gift of Wisdom.

18. *Catechism of the Catholic Church (CCC)*, no. 2607.

19. See *Summa theologiae* II-II q. 29, art. 1.

20. See Saint John of the Cross, *The Spiritual Canticle*, stanza 39, no. 2, in *The Collected Works of St. John of the Cross*, trans. K. Kavanaugh & O. Rodriguez (London: Thomas Nelson & Sons, 1964), p. 557.

21. See *Summa theologiae* II-II q. 188, art. 6: "Just as it is better to illumine than merely to shine, so it is better to give to others the things contemplated than simply to contemplate."

22. See John of the Cross, *Canticle*, stanza 39, no. 14.

23. For example, see his article on the nature of perfection in this life, *Summa theologiae* II-II q. 184, art. 2.

24. *Summa theologiae* II-II q. 46, art. 2.

25. For this characteristic teaching of Aquinas, see *Summa theologiae* II-II q. 45, art. 2.

26. *Summa theologiae* II-II q. 45, art. 6, ad 1.

27. See Bernard Gui, "The Life of St. Thomas Aquinas," no. 31.

28. Walz, *Luoghi*, p. 46.

29. Pierre Mandonnet, "Les titres doctoraux de saint Thomas d'Aquin," *Revue Thomiste* 17 (1909): 597–608, at 607: "Thomas a été angélique par ses vertus."

30. From the testimony at the first canonization inquiry of Peter of Montesangiovanni, in *The Life of Saint Thomas*, trans. & ed. Foster, p. 95.

31. Tocco, "Hystoria," p. 43, no. 12.

32. See *Summa theologiae* II-II q. 186, art. 4 & the *sed contra*. The noted expert on religious life, the late Father Jordan Aumann, o.p., offers this illuminating explanation of Aquinas's use of "perpetual continence" in his discussion of the perfection that religious life entails: "Thomas speaks of continence rather than chastity in regard to religious life because while the virtue of chastity allows for the moderate use of sexual pleasure in marriage continence

implies the abstention from all venereal pleasure and the firm will to resist the movements of fleshly concupiscence." See *The Pastoral and Religious Lives*, ed. Jordan Aumann, O.P., vol. 47 of the Blackfriars edition of Aquinas's *Summa Theologiae*, ed. Thomas Gilby (New York: McGraw-Hill, 1973), p. 114, note "a."

33. See *Summa theologiae* II-II q. 186, art. 4.

34. Ibid.

35. See, for instance, Aristotle's *Nicomachean Ethics*, Bk 3, 12 (1119b9).

36. *Summa theologiae* I q. 98, art. 2 & ad 2.

37. See *Summa theologiae* II-II q. 151, art. 1.

38. *Summa theologiae* II-II q. 153, art. 5.

39. *Summa theologiae* II-II q. 152, art. 2.

40. See *Summa theologiae* II-II q. 152, art. 5.

41. Jean-Pierre Torrell, O.P., *Saint Thomas Aquinas*, vol. 1, *The Person and His Work*, rev. ed., trans. Robert Royal (Washington, D.C.: The Catholic University of America Press, 2005), p. 27.

42. Torrell, *Thomas Aquinas*, p. 288, n. 101.

43. James A. Weisheipl, O.P., *Friar Thomas D'Aquino. His Life, Thought & Works* (Washington, D.C.: The Catholic University of America Press, 1983), p. 121.

44. Thomas Aquinas, "Sermon on the First Sunday after Epiphany," *Puer Jesus*, in *Thomas Aquinas: The Academic Sermons*, trans. Mark-Robin Hoogland, C.P. (Washington, D.C.: The Catholic University of America Press, 2010), p. 102.

45. *Summa theologiae* II-II q. 180, art. 2.

46. Ibid.

47. See *Summa theologiae* II-II q. 53, art. 5.

48. See *Summa theologiae* II-II q. 132, art. 2.

49. See *Summa theologiae* II-II q. 167, art. 1.

50. See *Summa theologiae* II-II q. 161, art. 1.

51. See *Summa theologiae* II-II q. 161, art. 2, ad 3.

52. Aquinas, *Academic Sermons*, (3.2.1), p. 102.

53. See Torrell, *Thomas Aquinas*, p. 9, for this account of the conclusion of the *Contra retrahentes*.

54. From the "Historia Ecclesiastica" of Tolomeo of Lucca, no. 24, in *The Life of Saint Thomas Aquinas: Biographical Documents*, trans. Kenelm Foster, o.p. (London: Longmans, Green and Co., 1959), p. 121.

55. Pope Urban IV published the bull *Transiturus* on 11 August 1264 and thus instituted the feast for the universal Church.

56. See *Summa theologiae* II-II q. 1, art. 7.

57. *Summa theologiae* II-II q. 1, art. 1 & q. 5, art. 3.

58. For a good explanation of this teaching and its relevance to contemporary issues in theology, see Colman E. O'Neill, o.p., "The Rule Theory of Doctrine and Propositional Truth," *The Thomist* 49 (1985), pp. 417–42.

59. *Summa theologiae* II-II q. 1, art. 2, ad 2.

60. For further discussion, see T. C. O'Brien, "Faith and the Truth about God," Appendix 3 of *Faith*, vol. 31 of the Blackfriars *Summa Theologiae* (New York: McGraw-Hill, 1975), pp. 195–201.

61. See a document of the Order of Preachers, *Constitutio Fundamentalis*, § II: "viri qui suam et aliorum salutem procurare desiderant."

62. *Regula Beati Augustini Episcopi*, no. 5: "Nec eant ad balnea, sive quocumque ire necesse fuerit, minus quam duo vel tres."

63. From Bernard Gui, "The Life of St. Thomas Aquinas," no. 31.

64. *CCC*, no. 144.

65. Pope John Paul II, Encyclical Letter, *Fides et ratio*, no. 43.

66. https://cantus.uwaterloo.ca/chant/681062

67. *Summa theologiae* II-II q. 180, art. 3, ad 1.

68. Cardinal Cajetan, *Commentary on Summa theologiae II-II q. 180*.